Original title:

Cozy Corners in Cold Weather

Copyright © 2024 Creative Arts Management OÜ

Author: Atticus Thornton
ISBN HARDBACK: 978-9916-94-464-6
ISBN PAPERBACK: 978-9916-94-465-3

## Whispers of Woolen Threads

In soft embrace, the fibers weave,
A tapestry of night's reprieve.
Whispers linger, tales unfold,
In woolen threads, the warmth we hold.

Silent shadows dance and spin,
As memories knit, where dreams begin.
Each stitch a secret, softly sewn,
A fabric rich with love we've known.

## Drift into the Warmth

When evening calls, the heart takes flight,
To cozy corners bathed in light.
With gentle sighs, the world will fade,
In golden hues, our fears betrayed.

Beneath the quilt, we snugly curl,
In whispers sweet, the night will twirl.
A warmth surrounds, like arms embraced,
In dreams we drift, our worries chased.

## Glistening Windows and Soft Hues

Through glistening panes, the day will glow,
As soft hues blend, in sunset's show.
The world outside begins to blur,
While inside hearts and hopes confer.

With gentle light, the shadows play,
In every color, night meets day.
Each moment framed, a memory hangs,
In silent whispers, the heart still sang.

## Soft Shadows and Sweet Reminiscence

In twilight's hush, shadows softly creep,
Where sweet reminiscence stirs from sleep.
Beneath the stars, old stories rise,
In whispered tones, under moonlit skies.

Each gentle breeze, a lover's sigh,
Brings echoes of laughter, sweet and nigh.
In soft embrace, we wander back,
Through time's warm glow, on memory's track.

## A Shimmering Pause in the Frost

Frozen crystals gleam so bright,
Winter whispers in the night.
Footprints lost beneath the snow,
Time takes pause, and gently flows.

Boughs weighed down in silver lace,
Nature's calm, a soft embrace.
Moments linger, hearts align,
In this stillness, peace we find.

## Fireside Melodies

Laughter dances in the glow,
Stories weave as embers flow.
Fingers warm, with cocoa stirred,
In this haven, dreams are heard.

Shadows playing on the wall,
In this warmth, we feel it all.
Voices join in sweet refrain,
Fireside songs soothe every vein.

## Time Stilled by the Hearth

Logs ablaze with crackling cheer,
Time stands still, the path is clear.
In the hearth, our thoughts ignite,
Moments cherished, pure delight.

Candles flicker, shadows dance,
In this space, we find romance.
Memories wrapped in fragrant air,
Time is stilled, we simply share.

## Hidden from the Whirlwind

Outside storms may howl and rage,
Inside we turn another page.
Together close, our worries cease,
In a bubble, we find peace.

The world outside may spin and sway,
Yet here, it's calm, come what may.
We'll hold tight through thick and thin,
In our haven, love will win.

## Scented Candles and Frosty Gaze

Softly glowing, winter's embrace,
Cinnamon whispers, a warm trace.
Frosty windows, a world at bay,
Scented candles guide our way.

Cardamom dreams and quiet cheer,
Hearts alight as candles near.
In the stillness, shadows dance,
Wrapped in warmth, we find romance.

## Chronicles Beneath the Eaves

Stories linger, as shadows play,
Whispers echo of yesterday.
Beneath the eaves, where secrets hide,
Chronicles told with hearts open wide.

Raindrops tap a timeless tune,
Ink and parchment, a tale to swoon.
Each line a bridge to distant lands,
Where dreams take flight from gentle hands.

## Hot Cocoa and Dreamy Escape

Frothy sweetness in each sip,
Cocoa warmth, a cozy trip.
Marshmallow clouds float above,
In this moment, we find love.

Snowflakes dance through twilight's glow,
As we drift where dreams do flow.
In every swirl, hopes intertwine,
With hot cocoa, your hand in mine.

## Hearthside Reveries

Crackling flames, a soothing sound,
In the hearth, our joy is found.
Stories shared in the amber light,
Hearthside reveries, pure delight.

Warmth encircles, the night is still,
Embers glow, hearts gently thrill.
In whispered dreams and glowing sights,
Together we weave our starry nights.

## Gentle Sighs of December

Whispers of snow on the ground,
Winter's breath softly found,
Trees stand bare, roots deep,
Secrets of silence they keep.

Frosty patterns on the pane,
Echoes of a past refrain,
As twilight gently descends,
Peace in the cold, heart mends.

Footsteps crunch on icy trails,
A hush where nature pales,
In the stillness, warmth will bloom,
Hope flourishes in winter's gloom.

## Warm Glow Against the Gray

Fireside crackles, stories told,
In the air, warmth unfolds,
Shadows dance on the wall,
Embers flicker, softly call.

Scarves wrapped tight against the breeze,
Laughter mingles with dark trees,
The world outside, a wisp of haze,
Yet here, we bask in golden rays.

Cocoa steams in hands held near,
Moments cherished, ever dear,
Outside it's bleak, yet inside glows,
A canvas where love freely flows.

## Moments of Solitude

Between the pages, silence speaks,
In the quiet, wisdom peaks,
A single chair by the fire,
Yearning for peace, hearts aspire.

Outside, the world spins with haste,
Within, a calm we seldom waste,
Thoughts like leaves begin to sway,
As we drift, hearts find their way.

Eyes closed, we breathe in deep,
Embracing the calm, secrets keep,
In solitude, we come alive,
In the stillness, we arrive.

## Candles in the Chill

Flickering lights in the night,
Casting warmth, a gentle light,
Against the cold, they softly glow,
Guiding hearts, as winds blow.

Shadows play on the walls,
While outside, the winter calls,
Together in this sacred space,
Finding comfort, our embrace.

Each flame a whisper of hope,
A reminder, together we cope,
In the chill, our spirits rise,
As we share in these gentle sighs.

### Frames of Felicity.

In the garden, flowers bloom bright,
Colors dance in the soft sunlight.
Laughter echoes, children play,
Moments cherished, day by day.

Time captured in a gentle frame,
Each smile speaks a cherished name.
Waves of joy, flowing free,
In this world, just you and me.

## Whispers of Warmth

Soft breezes carry secrets low,
Gentle murmurs in twilight's glow.
Under stars, hearts intertwine,
In whispers sweet, our souls align.

Embers crackle in the night,
Holding dreams, a flickering light.
With every sigh, a promise made,
In whispers of warmth, love won't fade.

### Snug Nooks in Frost

Winter blankets the world in white,
Frosty air plays with the light.
In snug nooks, we find our space,
Wrapped in warmth, a soft embrace.

The outside chill cannot invade,
By the fire, our fears allayed.
Cup of cocoa, stories shared,
In these moments, love declared.

## Hearthside Dreams

By the hearth, we sit and dream,
Firelight dances, a golden gleam.
Stories told of days gone by,
With every laugh, our spirits fly.

As shadows play upon the wall,
In this haven, we feel it all.
Hearthside warmth, our hearts aglow,
In these dreams, together we grow.

## Whispers of Warmth

In the glow of amber light,
Soft shadows dance with delight,
Laughter echoes through the air,
Love surrounds us everywhere.

Every crackle, every spark,
Tells a tale within the dark,
Hearts entwined in cozy cheer,
Whispers of warmth draw us near.

## Hearthside Musings

By the fire, thoughts take flight,
Memories blend with the night,
Each moment, a gentle sigh,
Time flows like the ember's eye.

Stories weave in soothing grace,
In this welcoming embrace,
Hearthside joys, a quiet song,
In togetherness we belong.

## Blanket of Serenity

Underneath a blanket's fold,
Gentle dreams begin to unfold,
Stars outside begin to gleam,
Wrapped in warmth, we softly dream.

A peaceful hush, the world asleep,
In our hearts, the memories deep,
With whispers soft as winter's breath,
We find solace, defying death.

## Fireside Reverie

Fireside glow, a world away,
Thoughts like embers come to play,
In the light, we share our fears,
In the warmth, we dry our tears.

Glimmers of hope in every crack,
In this moment, there's no lack,
Fireside dreams, we dare to chase,
In the stillness, we find grace.

## Embrace of the Chill

The winter winds begin to sigh,
All around, the snowflakes fly.
Blankets wrapped, we gather near,
In the hush, we conquer fear.

Breath steams rise into the night,
Stars above, so pure, so bright.
Nature's arms, both cold and clear,
In this stillness, we draw near.

# Sipping Tea by the Fire

The kettle sings, a soothing call,
As shadows dance upon the wall.
Clutching mugs of warmth and cheer,
Time slows down when loved ones are near.

The fire crackles, embers glow,
In every sip, the warmth does flow.
Whispers shared, sweet stories told,
In these moments, hearts unfold.

## Quietude in the Winter's Grasp

Silence echoes through the trees,
A peaceful space, a perfect freeze.
Frosty branches, nature's lace,
In this stillness, find your place.

Footsteps muffled on the ground,
In the hush, serenity found.
Winter's breath, a tender sigh,
Underneath the endless sky.

## Sheltered from the Storm

Raindrops patter on the roof,
In the house, we find our proof.
Warmth surrounds, the world outside,
In this cozy space, we hide.

Windows framed with frosted panes,
Nature's dance, the wind's refrains.
Together here, we brave the night,
In our hearts, we hold the light.

## Cradled in Softness

In quiet whispers, shadows blend,
Gentle sighs of day's slow end.
Softly wrapped in twilight's fold,
Dreams arise, both warm and bold.

Feathers float in dusky light,
Hushed embraces, peace takes flight.
Cradled close, the night is dear,
Safety found, with you near.

## Moments Uninterrupted by the Cold

Sunshine breaks the morning chill,
Radiance that makes time still.
A laugh escapes, the world feels warm,
In your gaze, it's always calm.

Branches sway with life's sweet song,
Where the heartache feels less strong.
Together, in this fleeting glow,
Moments pause, as soft winds blow.

## Retreating into Serene Spaces

In shadows deep, a refuge stands,
Embraced by nature's gentle hands.
Whispers rustle through the trees,
A harmony that brings us peace.

Time drifts slowly, thoughts unwind,
In quiet pools, serenity's kind.
Each breath a gift, each moment free,
Retreating where the soul can be.

## Snowfall and Serenity

Snowflakes dance on winter's breath,
Silent lands, a gentle depth.
Every flake, a story spun,
Blankets soft where dreams are won.

Peace envelops, the world turns white,
Softened edges, pure delight.
In the stillness, hearts take flight,
Snowfall wraps us, warm and bright.

# The Embrace of Steam

In morning's glow, the kettle sings,
A dance of warmth from gentle springs.
Steam rises high, a swirling fate,
Inviting whispers, a soft debate.

Each cup served forth, a soothing balm,
A moment's peace, a timeless calm.
The world outside, a distant dream,
Within the kitchen, we feel the steam.

Lavender scents on the briskened air,
Laughter lingers as we share.
With every sip, our spirits rise,
In the embrace of warmth, we surprise.

Golden light through window frames,
Flickers gently, stoking flames.
Together we bask, in every gleam,
Lost in the beauty of our steam.

## Winter's Softest Hugs

The snowflakes fall, a tender quilt,
Each flake a whisper, carefully built.
The chill outside, a frosty breath,
Yet close together, we know no death.

Blankets piled high, a snug delight,
We find our peace in cozy light.
Hot cocoa's warmth in every sip,
Wrapped in love, a gentle grip.

Frosted windows frame our view,
Winter's wonder, a world anew.
In hearty laughter and soft sighs,
The season's charm, a sweet surprise.

Outside we see the trees aglow,
Nature's art in the chill and snow.
But here inside, our hearts remain,
In winter's hugs, we feel no pain.

## Glimmers of Hearthlight

In the corner, the fire glows,
Casting warmth as evening flows.
Shadows dance on walls so bright,
Glimmers chase away the night.

The crackling logs, a soothing song,
Wrapped in warmth, where we belong.
The flicker of flame, a soft embrace,
Filled with wonder, time leaves no trace.

Each story shared, a cherished light,
Illuminating hearts, so bright.
Beneath the stars, the world seems small,
In our little space, we have it all.

A gentle hush as shadows drift,
Yearning whispers, love's true gift.
In the hearth's glow, we find our way,
Together, forever, come what may.

# Comfort Wrapped in Flannel

Soft flannel hugs against my skin,
Whispers of warmth inviting in.
Colors blend in the twilight hour,
Cocooned in fabric, we bloom like flowers.

With every thread, each gentle weave,
A cozy home where we believe.
Through storms and winds, we'll hold on tight,
Together we conquer the darkest night.

Books piled high, our evening's plan,
Lost in stories, time began.
The kettle sings from the stove so near,
Wrapped in flannel, we have no fear.

As seasons shift and daylight wanes,
In this embrace, our love remains.
True comfort found in every fold,
With flannel hugs, we are forever bold.

### Secrets of Softness

Whispers of the gentle night,
Embrace the dreams with tender light.
Feathers dance on silent air,
Secrets held in moments rare.

Every touch, a soft reply,
Cotton clouds drift in the sky.
Echoes of a lullaby,
Peaceful hearts, they never die.

In the corners, shadows play,
Nurtured hopes, they softly sway.
Gentle sighs and quiet tears,
Secrets wrapped throughout the years.

## Lullabies of Laughter

Bubbles rise with joyful sound,
Tickling toes upon the ground.
Songs of giggles fill the air,
Laughter weaves, a vibrant snare.

Moonlit games and fleeting days,
Hide and seek in playful maze.
Whispers of a childhood tune,
Chasing dreams beneath the moon.

Each chuckle matters, pure and bright,
Painting skies with colors light.
In this dance of joy, we find,
Laughter lingers in the mind.

# Nestled Beneath the Frost

Winter's breath, a silken shroud,
Nature whispers, soft and proud.
Blankets of white, a tranquil sight,
Nestled dreams in cozy light.

Footprints trace a path so clear,
Each step taken, joys draw near.
Frosted branches gleam and shine,
A world resting, calm, divine.

Inside warmth, a fire's dance,
Hearts entwined in timeless trance.
Winter's magic, soft and deep,
In the frost, our secrets keep.

# The Warmth We Create

Hands entwined, our laughter flows,
Beneath the sky, our spirits glow.
Candles flicker, shadows sway,
In this space, we find our way.

Stories shared with whispered bliss,
In every hug, a loving kiss.
Gathered close, we beat the cold,
Threads of warmth, a bond we hold.

Through stormy nights and brightest days,
In every heart, a fire stays.
Together we, through thick and thin,
The warmth we create, a sacred kin.

# Sipping Comfort by Candlelight

In a room lit soft and warm,
With shadows dancing, spirits charm.
A cup of warmth between my hands,
Whispers of peace in gentle strands.

The flicker of flame, a calming sight,
Outside the world fades into night.
Sipping slowly, letting time freeze,
Moments held close, like a sweet breeze.

Each sip a hug, a simple prayer,
In candle's glow, all burdens wear.
Comfort found in little things,
A refuge where my heart takes wing.

## Starlit Shelters

Above us spread a vast embrace,
Stars like lanterns, a cosmic grace.
Underneath this tapestry,
Dreams take flight, wild and free.

A blanket soft, wrapped tight around,
In this place, our hopes abound.
Silent wishes carried high,
To dance with clouds, to kiss the sky.

Each twinkle tells a tale of old,
Adventures whispered, secrets told.
In starlit shelters, hearts align,
In the infinite, we find the divine.

## Tales Told by the Fire

By the fire's glow, stories spin,
Of heroes lost and battles win.
With each crackle, a memory flares,
Echoes of laughter, ancient cares.

Flickering flames hold time in thrall,
Chasing shadows that rise and fall.
A world alive with words unfurled,
Each tale a key to a different world.

Gathered close, we lean in tight,
Wrapped in warmth, hearts ignite.
Voices dance in the amber light,
As tales unfold into the night.

## Melodies of Retreat

In quiet corners, whispers play,
Melodies of a slow decay.
Soft notes drift like autumn leaves,
Embrace the still, where sorrow cleaves.

The gentle strum of a weary heart,
Songs of solace, a work of art.
Each chord a balm for what we bear,
A lullaby that mends despair.

In the retreat, peace softly sighs,
In every note, a chance to rise.
Harmonics weave through every seam,
A tapestry of hope, a soothing dream.

# Nooks of Nectar

In hidden corners, blooms unfold,
The scent of sweetness, quiet and bold.
Honeyed whispers fill the air,
Nature's treasure, found with care.

Glimmers dance on petals bright,
Softly shimmering in the light.
A gentle hum, the bees have sung,
In nooks of nectar, life begun.

Colors splash on canvas green,
Life erupts where eyes are keen.
In every shadow, hope takes flight,
In secret spaces, pure delight.

Lost in wonder, heartbeats pulse,
A world unseen, a quiet convulse.
Here in the hush, sweet moments cling,
In nooks of nectar, love takes wing.

# Shadows and Soft Light

As twilight fades, shadows creep,
In tender hues, the moments seep.
Soft light dances on the ground,
Whispers of peace in silence found.

In every curve, the world slows down,
A gentle sigh, no need for sound.
Rich tones blend with the night's embrace,
In shadows soft, we find our place.

Beneath the stars, dreams take flight,
Wrapped in the arms of calm night.
A flicker here, a glow over there,
In shadows and soft light, love is rare.

Time drifts on, the heart feels free,
Setting our spirits wild, like the sea.
In the hush of dusk, a promise bright,
We find our way through shadows, to soft light.

# Embrace of the Evening

When day gives way to night's cool sigh,
The stars awake in the velvet sky.
Soft blankets wrap the world around,
In the embrace of evening, peace is found.

Crickets sing their twilight song,
A lullaby, gentle and long.
Moonlight weaves through branches bare,
In quiet moments, love is there.

The horizon blushes, a gentle grace,
A canvas painted, a warm embrace.
Night unveils its shimmering gown,
In the silence, worries drown.

Hold me close in the softening light,
Let our dreams take wing tonight.
In the embrace of the evening calm,
Find solace in this woven balm.

## Solace in Snug Spaces

Within the walls, a fortress stands,
In cozy nooks, we hold our plans.
Gentle light spills from windows wide,
In snug spaces, we choose to hide.

A fireplace flickers, stories told,
Wrapped in warmth, defenses hold.
Quiet murmurs and soft, sweet sighs,
In solace found, the spirit flies.

Pillows piled in fortresses high,
Nestled dreams beneath the sky.
Embraced by love, all fears erased,
In the calm of snug spaces, time is traced.

As twilight falls and shadows blend,
We find our peace, time to spend.
In these corners, hearts can race,
Discovering joy in snug spaces.

## Stillness Wrapped in Wool

In the corner, shadows bend,
Wrapped in warmth, time can mend.
Soft whispers of a distant night,
Cocooned in wool, the world feels right.

Fires flicker, embers glow,
Dreams weave softly, thoughts in tow.
Each stitch cradles a silent story,
In stillness, there's a hidden glory.

Through the window, frosts align,
Nature's canvas, pure design.
While outside, the world may freeze,
Inside, we hold a gentle peace.

# The Quietude of Nests

High among the swaying trees,
Nestled safe, protected ease.
Soft feathers line the gentle space,
A tranquil heart, a cozy place.

In whispered winds, the secrets dwell,
Of tiny lives, a soft-spoken spell.
Each twig and leaf a tale is spun,
Of rest and hope, where dreams are won.

As twilight falls, the shadows blend,
In quietude, where heartbeats mend.
Small beaks chirp a lullaby,
In nests of peace, beneath the sky.

## Plush Comfort Against the Cold

Winter's breath, a chilling sigh,
Yet in our hearts, the warmth can lie.
Plush blankets wrapped, a soothing shield,
Against the cold, our comfort's sealed.

Sipping tea, the steam ascends,
Each moment shared, love transcends.
A crackling fire dances bright,
In every flicker, pure delight.

Outside, the snowflakes gently fall,
While inside, we embrace it all.
Together, in this sacred space,
We find our warmth, our soft embrace.

## Flurries and Flickers


Outside, the flurries twirl and play,
In an endless dance of white ballet.
Shadows flicker, then disappear,
Creating magic, drawing near.

Candles glow, their flames alive,
In this moment, spirits thrive.
Whispers mingle with the winter night,
As stars above begin their flight.

Laughter echoes through the frost,
In cozy corners, warmth embossed.
Flurries fall, but hearts ignite,
In flickering dreams, we find our light.

# Wrapped in Stillness

In the hush of twilight's hour,
Whispers of peace gently flower.
Leaves dance softly, night extends,
Wrapped in stillness, all transcends.

Moonlight casts a silver glow,
Painting shadows, ebb and flow.
Hearts align in quiet grace,
In this moment, time we trace.

Branches sway beneath the stars,
Dreams unfold like open jars.
Silence sings a tender tune,
Holding secrets of the moon.

Breath held close, the world at bay,
In stillness, we find our way.
Wrapped in night, soft and deep,
In this silence, we shall keep.

## The Warmest Embrace

In the heart of winter's chill,
Love surrounds us, warm and still.
With every glance and gentle smile,
We embrace the world awhile.

Fingers intertwined in trust,
In the cold, our warmth is a must.
Laughter dances, spirits soar,
Every heartbeat, we want more.

Through frosted windows, light will gleam,
Hope ignites, a tender dream.
In this moment, time stands still,
Wrapped in warmth, we have our fill.

Let the storms of winter cry,
In our arms, we'll learn to fly.
The warmest embrace, ever true,
Just me and you, just me and you.

## Quietude in the Chill

In the quiet of the night,
Snowflakes drift, a soft delight.
Every breath a misty sigh,
In this chill, our dreams can fly.

Stars above begin to blink,
In the stillness, thoughts we think.
Nature whispers, tempting fate,
In the silence, we relate.

Branches bow beneath the weight,
In this moment, we create.
Frozen still, the world at rest,
Within us lies a gentle zest.

Quietude wraps like a dream,
In the dusk, our souls will beam.
Embrace the chill; find the peace,
In this tranquil space, release.

# Candles in the Cold

Flickering lights in darkest night,
Candles shine, bringing delight.
Against the cold, they bravely glow,
In their warmth, hopes start to grow.

Each flame tells a silent tale,
Of love and joy that will not pale.
Softly dancing, shadows play,
In their glow, we wish to stay.

In every flicker, dreams ignite,
Candles spark the purest light.
Holding fast against the freeze,
With each breath, our hearts find ease.

In the cold, a sanctuary,
Candles hum a sweet memory.
Together here, we stand so bold,
In the warmth of candles' hold.

## Mugs and Memories

In a cozy nook, we sipped our tea,
Laughter echoed sweetly, wild and free.
The warmth of mugs cradled in our hands,
Sharing secrets, dreams, and future plans.

Steam swirls danced like thoughts in flight,
In that moment, everything felt right.
Your smile brightened the cool, grey day,
Mugs held memories, both blissful and gay.

Time slipped softly, like sugar in brew,
Every sip savored, more than just two.
Each drop we shared tasted of delight,
Bound in friendship, our hearts were light.

Mugs now empty, the day must end,
Yet in my heart, you'll always blend.
Memories linger like sweet aftertaste,
In our next meeting, there's no time to waste.

## Inked Pages Underneath the Glow

Underneath a lamp's gentle glow,
Whispers of tales begin to flow.
Inked pages hold dreams yet to weave,
Stories waiting for us to believe.

The click of pens, an orchestra's tune,
Sketching thoughts while dust dances with moon.
Pages flutter like wings in the night,
Capturing moments, a dance of light.

Journals cradle secrets, hopes untold,
In every scribble, a treasure of gold.
Ink will shimmer like stars that gleam,
In this quiet space, we dare to dream.

Open the pages, let the stories unfold,
Underneath the glow, let destinies mold.
With every word, we create and connect,
Inked pages serve, as a bridge to reflect.

## Bundled Journeys

Wrapped tight in slumber, dreams take flight,
Adventures await beyond the night.
Bundled in layers, against the chill,
Each step we take, our hearts will thrill.

Mountains call, with whispers so bold,
Paths yet trodden, and stories untold.
With every journey, we shed and grow,
Bundled in laughter, we bask in the glow.

Through forest trails or cityscape hues,
Our footprints blend in vibrant views.
Together we wander, hand in hand,
Exploring the beauty of this vast land.

At day's end, under starlit skies,
We gather 'round, sharing our sighs.
Bundled close, in warmth we reside,
Every journey cherished, as hearts collide.

## Huddled Warmth in Winter's Thrall

In winter's chill, we find our grace,
Huddled close in a warm embrace.
Frosted windows, a breath of white,
Inside we glow, hearts illumined bright.

The crackling fire speaks in low tones,
Whispers of comfort, like familiar bones.
Cup of cocoa, marshmallows afloat,
Each sip a hug, a tender note.

Blankets wrap us, a fortress snug,
Stories linger, laughter and shrug.
Outside the world is lost in snow,
But here, in our warmth, love continues to grow.

As night deepens, the stars gleam above,
In winter's thrall, we find our love.
Huddled together, we brave the cold,
With every moment, new memories unfold.

## Heartfelt Cheers in the Nipping Wind

In the chilly breeze, we gather near,
Voices raised high, our laughter clear.
Frost on our cheeks, a warm embrace,
In the nipping wind, we find our place.

With cups held high, we toast the night,
Stars twinkle softly, a stunning sight.
The warmth of friendship wraps us tight,
Heartfelt cheers under the moonlight.

A crackling fire, we share our dreams,
In every whisper, excitement beams.
Through the cold air, our spirits rise,
Heartfelt cheers beneath the skies.

This moment cherished, forever held,
In the nipping wind, our stories meld.
Together we stand, no fear, no dread,
Heartfelt cheers as our souls are fed.

# The Joy of Being Still

In quiet moments, life unfolds,
Silent whispers, tales untold.
A gentle pause, a soothing sigh,
The joy of being still, oh my!

Leaves dance lightly, shadows play,
The world slows down, in soft decay.
Breathing in peace, with a tranquil heart,
In stillness we find a brand new start.

Birds sing softly, a lullaby sweet,
Nature's rhythm, a calming beat.
In the quiet, thoughts drift and sway,
The joy of being still leads the way.

With time suspending, worries cease,
In stillness, we find our inner peace.
Each moment savored, like morning dew,
The joy of being still, always true.

## Footsteps in Fresh Snow

A blanket white, so pure and bright,
Footsteps scatter in the soft twilight.
Each crunch beneath, a melody sweet,
Footsteps in fresh snow, winter's treat.

The world transforms, a serene scene,
Quiet beauty, pure and clean.
With every step, a story shared,
Footsteps in fresh snow, gently bared.

Laughter echoes in the crisp air,
Joy bundled up, without a care.
We dance and twirl, letting spirits flow,
Footsteps in fresh snow, watch us go!

As twilight falls, the stars will gleam,
In winter's embrace, we live our dream.
These footprints tell of where we roam,
Footsteps in fresh snow, we find a home.

## Daydreams by the Glowing Hearth


By the glowing hearth, tales unwind,
Flickering flames, peace we find.
In warmth we linger, wrapped in light,
Daydreams dance in the soft twilight.

Conversations flow, like rivers wide,
Hearts open up, no need to hide.
With every crackle, new dreams take flight,
Daydreams by the hearth, a soothing sight.

Memories made, we share and create,
In this cozy space, we celebrate.
The world outside, so cold and vast,
Daydreams by the hearth, forever cast.

As shadows grow long, our laughter swells,
In every story, a magic dwells.
Together we sit, as the stars align,
Daydreams by the glowing hearth, divine.

## Tapestries of Comfort and Light

We weave our dreams in twilight's glow,
Threads of memory in soft, warm flow.
Colors blend where laughter spins,
In every corner, cherished kin.

Gentle whispers in the night,
Embracing hearts in pure delight.
Each stitch a tale, each knot a sigh,
In this safe haven, love won't die.

Together we craft a vibrant scene,
With hopes and wishes in every seam.
The world outside may fade away,
But here, in comfort, we choose to stay.

As dawn approaches with golden rays,
We savor warmth in the afterglow of days.
Tapestries woven through laughter and tears,
Holding us close through the years.

# The Stillness of Sipping Slowly


In a porcelain cup, warmth begins,
Steam rises softly, the day now thins.
Thoughts linger sweetly on each sip,
Time stretches gently as moments slip.

The world outside rushes by in haste,
But here I linger, savoring taste.
Each drop a pause, a breath, a sigh,
In this stillness, peace can lie.

Silken leaves dance in swirling brew,
A symphony of flavors rich and true.
The clock stands still while I embrace,
This simple pleasure, this quiet space.

With every sip, the worries fade,
A tranquil heart in the warmth conveyed.
In this ritual, I find my way,
The stillness of sipping takes me away.

## Evening Shadows and Warmth

As daylight wanes, shadows play,
Lighting fires with the end of day.
Soft ember glow, a dance of light,
Whispers of warmth in the approaching night.

Outside, the stars begin to gleam,
Inside, we wrap in cozy dream.
Stories shared in flickering flame,
Each moment cherished, never the same.

Blankets pulled close, we laugh and sigh,
With every flicker, the worries fly.
Evening's embrace, a gentle caress,
In your presence, I find my rest.

With shadows deep and spirits bright,
We gather close, held by the night.
In every heartbeat, the warmth flows through,
Evening shadows, a dance born anew.

# Storytelling by the Hearthside

Crackling logs in the fireplace glow,
Flickering tales from long ago.
In the circle of light, we gather near,
Each voice a melody, perfectly clear.

Adventures unfold with every breath,
Echoes of laughter blend with death.
Weaving dreams in the warmth of the flame,
A tapestry rich with love and the same.

Children wide-eyed, lean in to hear,
Roots of our history become quite near.
Every story a thread to bind,
Hearts intertwined, comforts aligned.

Together we journey, in time and space,
In the hearth's embrace, we find our place.
With each ending, another dawn,
Storytelling lives, and we carry on.

## A Whispered Embrace

In twilight's hush, the shadows play,
Soft secrets shared, as night turns day.
A breeze entwines the dreams we weave,
In whispered tones, our hearts believe.

Beneath the stars, our souls entwined,
With every sigh, the world aligned.
A gentle touch, a knowing glance,
In silence found, we take our chance.

Every heartbeat, a tender song,
In this embrace, we both belong.
With quiet strength, we stand as one,
In whispered love, our fears undone.

As dawn breaks bright, we'll softly trace,
The memories made in this embrace.
Forever held, in moments dear,
A whispered love, forever near.

# Gathering of Hearts

Underneath the old oak's shade,
We gather close, our worries fade.
In laughter's warmth, the world feels light,
A gathering of hearts, pure delight.

With stories shared, the past unfolds,
In fleeting moments, friendship holds.
The ties that bind can never sever,
In each embrace, we're strong forever.

The setting sun paints skies aglow,
In every smile, the love we sow.
Together here, we find our place,
In this sweet dance, a tender grace.

As night descends, our voices blend,
A symphony that knows no end.
In joyful hearts, we'll always stay,
In this gathering, come what may.

# Tranquil Tides of Winter

Upon the shore, the winter's breath,
In crystal waves that whisper death.
The moonlight glimmers on icy seas,
A tranquil hush, the world at ease.

As snowflakes fall with gentle grace,
Each flake a dream, a soft embrace.
The silent nights, so deep and clear,
In winter's warmth, our hearts draw near.

With every tide that ebbs and flows,
A soothing balm, the stillness grows.
In chilling winds, we find a song,
A rhythm sweet where we belong.

As morning breaks with hues of gold,
The winter's tale begins to unfold.
In tranquil tides, life's beauty lies,
A peaceful heart beneath the skies.

# Beneath the Warming Glow

Beneath the stars, we sit and dream,
The world aglow with gentle beams.
In laughter shared, our spirits rise,
A warming glow that never dies.

In golden hues, the sun will set,
A promise held, we'll not forget.
With hands held tight, and hearts aflame,
In this embrace, we'll forge our name.

As shadows dance, the night unfolds,
With whispered tales, and secrets told.
In every spark, a moment's grace,
Together here, we find our place.

With starlit skies and dreams in tow,
We'll wander where the wild winds blow.
In love's embrace, we'll always stand,
Beneath the glow, forever hand in hand.

## Meeting the Cold with Warmth

In the heart of winter's chill,
Fires crackle, hearts do fill.
Blankets wrapped, we gather close,
In the warmth, our spirits boast.

Frosty breath dances in the air,
Yet inside, we have naught but care.
Laughter echoes, bright and clear,
Together, banishing the fear.

Hands entwined, we forge a bond,
Amidst the cold, we truly respond.
With every hug, a glow ignites,
In our haven, love ignites.

As snowflakes fall, so soft and light,
We shield our souls, holding tight.
Meeting the cold with warmth around,
In unity, true joy is found.

# A Kaleidoscope of Comfort

In patches bright, the world unfolds,
A tapestry of stories told.
Colors mingle, warmth abounds,
In every corner, comfort sounds.

Gentle whispers of the trees,
And the fluttering of leaves in the breeze.
Every shade a tender embrace,
A kaleidoscope of healing grace.

Sipping tea as shadows play,
Moments linger, drift away.
In these hues, we find our place,
Wrapped in softness, we embrace.

With every dawn, new light to chase,
Through every shift, we find our space.
A spectrum bright in life's sweet seam,
We weave together, share the dream.

## Windows Framed by Frost

Framed in ice, the world outside,
Views transformed, the warmth we bide.
Patterns lace the glass with grace,
Inside, the hearth's inviting space.

Each pane a canvas, winter's art,
Whispering tales that warm the heart.
As firelight dances, shadows play,
A cozy refuge from the day.

Beneath the frost, life stirs anew,
Silent magic, soft and true.
With every breath, a fleeting glimpse,
Of nature's beauty, awe it wimps.

Through windows clear, we glimpse a spark,
As winter sings its timeless arc.
In the stillness, peace we find,
Framed in frost, yet warm in mind.

# Rejuvenation of the Spirit

From deep within, the light will rise,
Awakening dreams beneath the skies.
In nature's arms, we find our core,
Rejuvenation, a vibrant lore.

Through daily trials, we often tread,
Yet hope ignites when darkness spreads.
With every dawn, new paths to blur,
In whispered winds, the spirits stir.

Moments linger, sweet and blessed,
In solitude, we find our rest.
A gentle heart, a knowing soul,
In harmony, we become whole.

As seasons shift and time unfolds,
The spirit dances, brave and bold.
Rejuvenation, a cherished art,
In every beat, a brand-new start.

# A Cup of Tranquility

Steam rises slow, a gentle swirl,
In quiet moments, life unfurls.
With each sip, the world grows still,
In a cup of peace, my heart can fill.

Soft whispers wrap like fading light,
Comfort found in the depths of night.
A taste of calm, a fleeting thought,
In this warm brew, solace is caught.

Outside the storm, a distance away,
Inside, the warmth keeps cold at bay.
With every drop, a story shared,
In every moment, love is bared.

So here I sit, my mind at ease,
In the simple pleasures, I find peace.
A cup to hold, a heart to mend,
In tranquil sips, I find my friend.

# Winter's Gentle Nook

In winter's grasp, the world sleeps tight,
A gentle nook, where day meets night.
Snowflakes dance on the whispering breeze,
Nature's blanket wraps all with ease.

Warmth of the fire, a flicker of gold,
Stories unfold as the night grows old.
The chill outside can't penetrate,
In cozy corners, we find our fate.

Footprints in snow, a fleeting trace,
Time slows down in this quiet space.
In stillness found, our spirits soar,
In winter's nook, we crave for more.

With hearts aglow and laughter bright,
We share our dreams in the fading light.
Together we sit, embrace the cold,
In winter's love story, we are bold.

# Hidden Havens of Heat

Beneath the stars, where secrets dwell,
Warmth embraces like a wishing well.
In pockets of light, where hearts ignite,
Hidden havens shelter the night.

Flickering flames dance, shadows play,
Softly they whisper, guiding the way.
Together we gather, souls intertwined,
In moments of magic, peace is defined.

The chill retreats, as laughter flows,
In every glance, affection grows.
Beneath the moon's soft and radiant gaze,
Hidden havens, in a soft haze.

With every heartbeat, warmth bestowed,
In treasured spaces, love's seeds are sowed.
Together we bask in friendship's glow,
In hidden havens, our spirits grow.

## Flickers and Fables

In flickers of light, tales are spun,
Of heroes and journeys, races won.
Around the fire, stories ignite,
Fables whispered in the quiet night.

With every spark, a vision blooms,
From shadows rise, creativity looms.
A tapestry woven with dreams and fears,
In the warm embrace, laughter adheres.

The flickering flames dance with grace,
Each story shared finds its place.
In the heart of night, where wonders dwell,
Flickers and fables cast a spell.

In every corner, a memory lives,
Inshared moments, the heart forgives.
We gather close, in unity bold,
Flickers of warmth, fables retold.

# Tales Woven by Hearthlight

In the glow of the flame's warm embrace,
Stories unfold, each face finds its place.
Whispers of old drift through the night,
Hearthlight dances, casting shadows bright.

We gather close, hearts beating as one,
Tales of adventure when daylight is done.
The crackle of wood, the warmth of the fire,
Moments shared, lifting spirits higher.

Memories linger, a tapestry spun,
In flickering light, our laughter still runs.
Each tale a thread, in this cozy domain,
Woven together, joy mixed with pain.

So let us delight in the hearth's soft glow,
With love and light, let our hearts freely flow.
For in this warmth, we find our true kin,
Tales woven by hearthlight, a world to begin.

## Nestled Amongst Illumination

Beneath the stars, in the still of the night,
We nestle close, hearts filled with delight.
Glimmers of hope dance in our eyes,
Illumination surrounds, chasing the sighs.

In the gentle breeze, soft whispers we send,
Sharing our dreams, our souls start to mend.
The world falls away as we breathe in the light,
Nestled together, our spirits take flight.

Moments like these, pure treasure we find,
Illuminated paths that once were confined.
With every heartbeat, new horizons appear,
Nestled amongst glow, we conquer our fear.

So let the night wrap us, tender and near,
In this embrace, we have nothing to fear.
Amidst the illumination, our spirits shall soar,
Together forever, we seek to explore.

# A Sanctuary from the Storm

Raindrops patter on the window pane,
A sanctuary found, away from the rain.
With every gust that rattles the door,
Inside we are safe, our hearts evermore.

In the tempest's howl, we find our release,
Wrapped in warmth, enveloped in peace.
The storm may rage, but we stand as one,
A bond forged in fire, till the night is done.

We sip our tea as the winds start to wane,
Sharing our stories, our dreams uncontained.
Outside the chaos, but here we remain,
A sanctuary from which hope shall not drain.

So let the winds howl, let the thunder roll,
Within these walls, we shelter the soul.
A refuge where love gently keeps us warm,
Together we'll weather, through any storm.

## Reprieve in the Frosty Air

Under a blanket of shimmering white,
We stroll through the shadows, in soft moonlight.
Breath visible, floating like dreams in the night,
Reprieve in the frosty air feels just right.

Snowflakes flutter, like whispers of grace,
Each step crunches softly, a slow-paced embrace.
With every breath, the world slows down,
In stillness, we dance, as snow starts to crown.

Winter's chill wraps us, tender and tight,
In this moment, everything feels bright.
The stars overhead twinkle, a celestial rare,
Sharing their magic in the frosty air.

So let us wander, in this frozen land,
With hearts intertwined, and fingers fanned.
In the beauty of winter, we find our own flare,
A reprieve together, in the crisp evening air.

## A Blanket of Comfort

Softly it falls, the snow so white,
Wrapping the world in gentle light.
A comforting hush, a serene embrace,
Nature dons her wintery lace.

Children's laughter fills the air,
Building their dreams without a care.
The warmth of hearts, the chill outside,
In this blanket of comfort, we all confide.

Fires crackle in the hearth's warm glow,
Tales shared by friends as the breezes blow.
Mugs of cocoa, a sweet delight,
Together we bask in the winter night.

So let it snow, let the storm rage on,
We find our peace till the break of dawn.
Wrapped in love, through cold we strive,
In a blanket of comfort, we truly thrive.

# Warmth Beneath Winter's Veil

Beneath the frost, the earth does dream,
A hidden warmth, a gentle gleam.
Life slumbers deep, yet stirs within,
Waiting for spring to begin again.

The sky grows dim, the stars take flight,
Winter's hand brings the longest night.
But in the silence, hope does weave,
A fabric of life that we believe.

With every flake that graces the ground,
A promise whispers, softly profound.
The warmth beneath, a truth to trust,
Emerging from shadows, in light we must.

Time will pass, the cold will flee,
Nature's canvas, a symphony.
Embrace the chill, for soon you'll see,
Warmth beneath winter's veil, set free.

## Flickering Shadows on Snow

Moonlight dances on a sea of white,
Casting shadows that twinkle at night.
The world transformed, a magical sight,
Flickering whispers in the still twilight.

Trees adorned in crystal lace,
Hold secrets of winter's embrace.
Each branch a story, each flake a song,
In this wonderland, we all belong.

Footprints traced in a quilted crust,
Memories created, in laughter we trust.
The flickering flames in the distance glow,
Guiding us homeward through the snow.

So let the shadows play and roam,
As frost paints pictures, we find our home.
In the quiet night, our hearts will know,
The beauty lies in the flickering glow.

# Refuge in the Frostbite

In the heart of winter, a chill does bite,
Nature rests in the frost's pure light.
Yet in this cold, we find a spark,
A refuge built within the dark.

Sweaters bundled, hands held tight,
Sharing stories through the long night.
The world seems harsh, but we stand near,
Finding warmth where love is clear.

Outside the winds may howl and scrape,
But inside, dreams take joyous shape.
With laughter echoing, shouts of glee,
In our refuge, we're wild and free.

So let the frost dance on each pane,
We'll cherish moments in joy and pain.
Through every storm, no need to fight,
For we have refuge in the frostbite.

## A Warm Chair's Embrace

In the corner, shadows play,
A gentle light guides the way.
Soft fabric wraps around me tight,
In this chair, all feels right.

The world outside can bluster and roar,
But here, I need nothing more.
In a cocoon of warmth, I stay,
Dreaming the troubles away.

A book rests open upon my knee,
Whispers of tales from lands I see.
Time drifts softly like a feather,
In my warm chair, light as a tether.

Slippers hug my weary feet,
This is where solace feels complete.
With a sigh, I find my peace,
In this warm chair, my worries cease.

## Tucked Away from the Chill

Winter winds howl outside,
But in here, I can hide.
Wrapped in blankets, snug and tight,
This refuge feels just right.

The frost paints on every pane,
While the hearth flickers with flame.
Cocoa warms my hands, so sweet,
Every sip a cozy treat.

The world is white, a silent song,
Yet in this warmth, I belong.
Shadows dance upon the wall,
Here, I find joy in it all.

Moments linger, slow and bright,
In this haven from the night.
I smile, knowing I am safe,
Tucked away in this warm space.

## Chasing the Echo of a Crackling Fire

The fire crackles, soft and low,
Its warmth a dance, a gentle glow.
Pine wood snaps, a joyful sound,
In its embrace, solace is found.

Shapes in flames twist and sway,
Whispering stories of yesterday.
Memories flicker with each spark,
Filling the room, brightening the dark.

A trance in the heat, I sit and stare,
Chasing echoes through the air.
Each snap, each pop, a voice from the past,
Reminding me of moments that last.

In the glow, I lose my way,
Finding comfort in the play.
The fire's spirit, wild and free,
Keeps me warm, eternally.

## Tea Leaves and Frosted Glass

Steam rises, curling in the air,
Mingling with the winter's stare.
A teapot whistles, soft and clear,
Bringing comfort, drawing near.

Frosted glass, a world on pause,
Outside, nature's mellow laws.
Within these walls, everything's bright,
With tea leaves blooming, pure delight.

Sipping warmth from my favorite cup,
The magic in flavors, I drink it up.
Each sip a story, ancient and wise,
In this moment, time gently flies.

The sun sets low with a gentle grace,
Painting the room in its embrace.
Tea leaves dance and softly tease,
In this warmth, my spirit's ease.

## The Allure of Warmth

In shadows deep, the embers glow,
A secret pull, a tender flow.
The soft embrace of cozy nights,
A whispering kiss, where peace ignites.

Beneath the blanket, dreams take flight,
Chasing away the fear of night.
A gentle hearth, where spirits mend,
In warmth's embrace, our hearts transcend.

The world outside, a chilling dread,
Yet here we light the warmth we spread.
With laughter shared, the moments spark,
In love's embrace, we leave our mark.

So let us bask in golden rays,
Together here, through endless days.
The allure of warmth, forever near,
In every heartbeat, filled with cheer.

# Retiring from the Chill

As daylight fades, the frost draws near,
We seek the glow, we crave the cheer.
With scarves wrapped tight, we roam no more,
Inside our haven, secure and sure.

The windows fog with laughter bright,
Our breaths release, a dance of light.
Hot cocoa warms our frozen hands,
While winter's bite seals frosty lands.

With stories told, the night unfolds,
In whispered tones, our hearts, they hold.
Retiring from the cold's cruel bite,
In honesty shared, we find delight.

So let the chill prevail outside,
We'll find our refuge, side by side.
As firelight flickers, spirits rise,
In warmth's embrace, the world defies.

# Mingling with the Firelight

The crackling flame, a timeless song,
In quiet corners, where we belong.
The flicker dances, shadows sway,
As magic weaves through night and day.

Each spark that flies, a wish in flight,
With dreams ignited by the light.
We gather close, with hearts aglow,
In fire's embrace, the warmth will flow.

Stories whispered, old and new,
By firelight's hue, friendships grew.
Mingling laughter with the heat,
In this haven, life feels complete.

So let the world outside grow dim,
In this warm glow, we'll never skim.
Together, we seize each fleeting night,
In bonds of love, we find our light.

## Serene Evenings in the Bluster

The wind may howl, the snow may fall,
Yet inside here, we heed the call.
With candles lit, the shadows play,
In serene peace, we drift away.

The world outside, a tempest wild,
Yet here we sit, with hearts beguiled.
Wrapped in warmth, our spirits rise,
As winter whispers through the skies.

With every gust, we hold each close,
In tranquil moments, love engrosses.
Serene evenings in the bluster bright,
We find our calm in the darkest night.

So let the storms rage fierce and free,
For here together, we will be.
In cozy nooks, our dreams will dance,
In warmth and love, we take our chance.